Things to make for Christmas

D0785632

Things to make for Christmas

Eric Kenneway

Illustrated by Jane Laycock

Beaver Books

A Beaver Book
Published by Arrow Books Limited
62 – 65 Chandos Place, London WC2N 4NW

An imprint of Century Hutchinson Limited

London Melbourne Sydney Auckland
Johannesburg and agencies throughout the world

First published 1985
Reprinted 1985 (twice)

Text © Eric Kenneway 1985
Illustrations © Hutchinson Publishing Group 1985

Set in Linoterm Baskerville

Printed and bound in Great Britain by
Anchor Brendon Ltd, Tiptree, Essex

ISBN 0 09 938140 0

Contents

Foreword

Here is a collection of ideas on things to do for Christmas — ways of decorating your room; how to make greeting cards and simple gifts as well as the fancy papers in which to wrap them. There are also a few ideas on making Christmassy things to eat.

One word of warning: do not be half-hearted with your decorations — a paper chain can look very sad and lonely hanging by itself. Make plenty of them. They will not take very long to make if two or three of you get together.

Before starting work on your decorations, it is a good idea to invest in a pocket stapler if you do not have one already. You may be able to manage by sticking your pieces together with paste or glue, but paper chains and other decorations will be stronger and less likely to fall apart if they are stapled together. Staplers and packets of staples can be found in many little general shops as well as in stationery shops.

So now you are ready to start. Here's wishing you a Merry Christmas — and a very busy one.

Paper chains

One or two newspapers will provide you with enough material to decorate a whole room if you cut them into the sort of paper chain described below. Before you start making the chains, you may like to take a big brush and paint stripes, or just patches of colour, on the paper you mean to use. This will make your paper chains more colourful.

Of course, when you have tried out the various methods in newspaper, you can then employ the same methods with more expensive paper or with fancy paper described on pages 79–92.

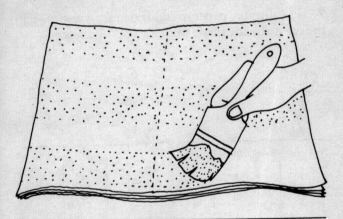

Moorish paper chain

You will need: strips of paper, about 10cm (4 ins) wide
scissors
staples or glue

1 Make cuts, 2–3cm apart, into one side of the paper. Do not take the cuts too close to the opposite edge.

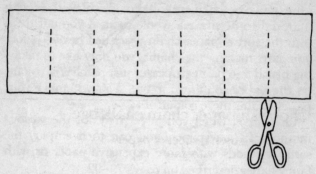

2 Now turn the paper round and make cuts between the ones already made from the opposite side.

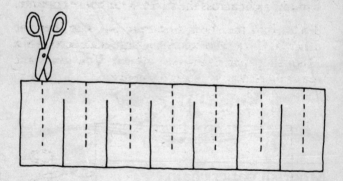

3 Take hold of the ends and pull apart. You'll find you have a chain of Moorish arches with pointed tops. Make several strips of these arches and staple or glue the ends together.

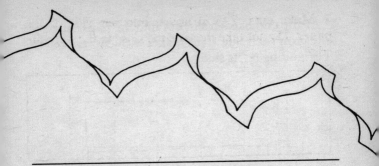

Moorish paper chain challenge

You will need: a sheet of paper
                    scissors

It can be interesting to see how long a strip you can make from a single sheet of paper without glueing or stapling. You might like to see if you can make a page from a newspaper stretch, say, from your bedroom window right across the street to the house opposite.

1 Cut into the sheet, first from one side then the other, as if you were making a large-scale section of a Moorish paper chain (see above). You can make many more than two cuts if you like.

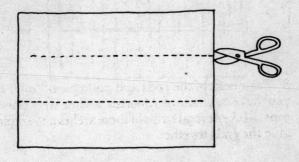

2 At the end of each slit, cut into the paper at right angles on each side. This makes each cut resemble a 'T' standing on its side.

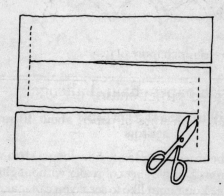

3 Then treat each flap as a separate strip and cut into this too, as for the Moorish paper chain.

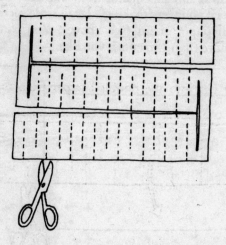

4 When you open up the paper, you will find it looks like this:

but there is much more of it.

Perforated paper chain

You will need: strips of paper, about 10cm (4ins) wide
scissors

1 First fold a strip of paper in half.

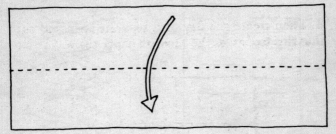

2 Then cut into the doubled paper from top and bottom.

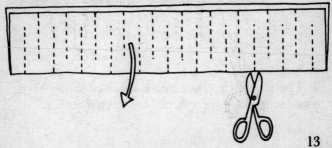

3 Open up the paper and pull the ends apart.

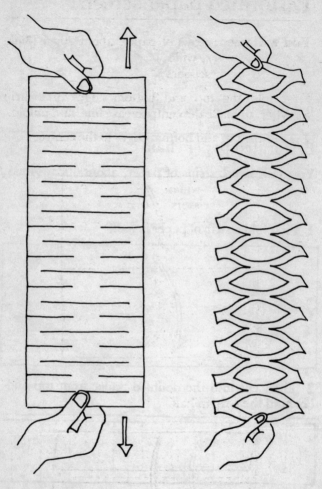

4 The paper stretches into a series of loops. Make more sections and staple or glue them together.

Perforated paper screen

You will need: strips of paper, about 20cm (8ins) wide

scissors

First fold the top and bottom edges of a strip together, to make the centre crease line, and unfold.

1 Fold the top and bottom edges to the centre.

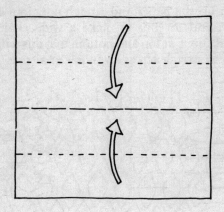

2 Fold the strip in half.

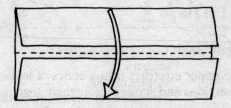

3 Cut through the layers of paper from the top and the bottom.

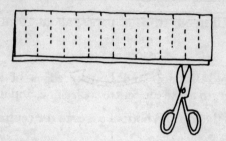

4 Open up the paper and stretch out. Join several sections, end to end, to make a wide chain. Try joining sections at top and bottom too; this will make a screen to stretch across a window or alcove.

Lanterns

You will need: two squares of paper
scissors
staples or glue
a needle and thread (optional)

1 Start by folding a square of paper in half. With the fold at bottom, fold from left to right.

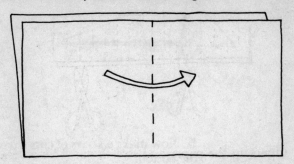

2 Then fold the left edge to the bottom edge . . .

3 . . . and the diagonal fold to the bottom edge. Turn the paper over . . .

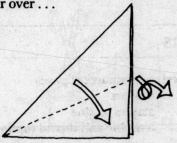

4 . . . and cut off the triangular area at left.

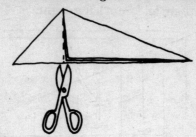

5 Now make a series of cuts from the bottom . . .

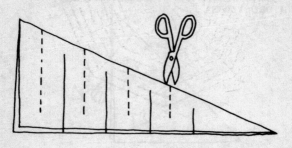

6 . . . and a series of cuts from the top – just as you did when making the paper chains (pages 9–16).

7 Carefully separate all the layers and open up.

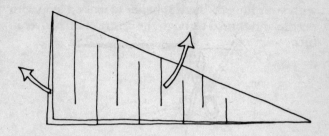

8 Make a similar shape by folding and cutting your second sheet of paper. Lay one on top of the other and fasten them together with a stapler at each corner marked with an X in the drawing.

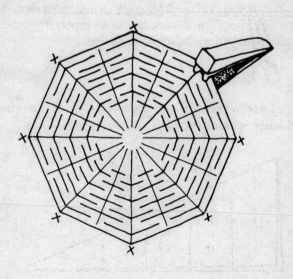

9 Now stretch the flat form into a lantern by pulling the two centres apart. You may be able to do this with your fingers, but it is better to make a loop with needle and thread through the centre of each layer in turn.

10 When you pull on the threads, the lantern should open like this. The decoration looks especially good when displayed with the paper chains.

Paper balls

You will need: an old colour magazine
a pencil
scissors
staples
a saucer

1 Place a saucer upside-down on an old magazine. Draw a line around the saucer's edge. Remove the saucer and cut around the line through five pages to make five paper discs.

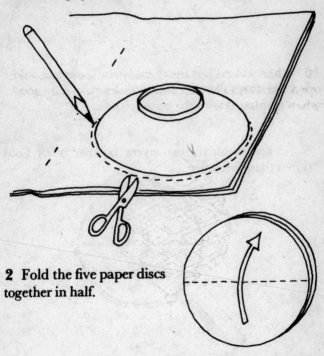

2 Fold the five paper discs together in half.

3 Staple neatly just above the folded edge at left and right. Fold down the uppermost layer.

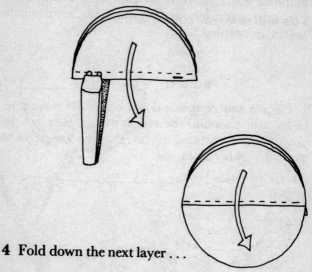

4 Fold down the next layer . . .

5 . . . and staple the two layers together at left. Fold down the third layer . . .

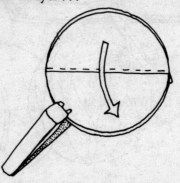

6 . . . and staple this to the layer beneath at right. Continue to fold down one layer of paper at a time, stapling each in turn to the layer immediately beneath alternately at left and right, until all the layers are stapled . . .

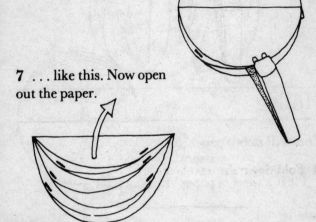

7 . . . like this. Now open out the paper.

8 You will find you have made a decorative half-ball. You can use this as a wall decoration between festoons of paper chains.

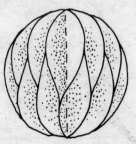

9 Staple two half-balls together to make one complete ball.

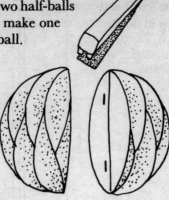

Holly

You will need: paper
scissors

1 Pleat a sheet of paper into quarters . . .

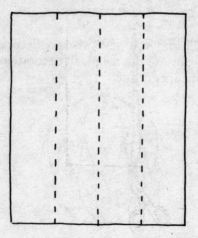

2 . . . like this. Then fold
in half from top to bottom.

3 Cut two fat curves through all layers from one
corner to that diagonally opposite. Unfold the
paper . . .

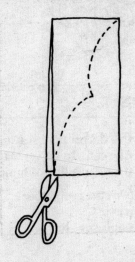

4 . . . and you have a holly leaf. Make several and group them with paper balls (page 21) to serve as berries. Pin the holly leaves on the wall with drawing-pins and suspend the 'berries' from some pins with thread.

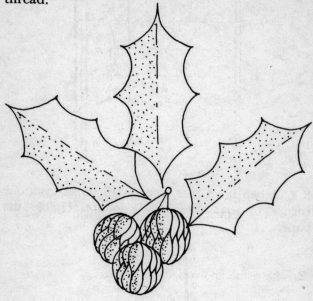

Fan flowers

Some people see this decoration as a star and some a sunburst. It could be called a flower. Make several so that they can be strung in a line or hung in groups.

You will need: two sheets of paper
scissors
staples or glue

1 Pleat a sheet of paper into eighths. Do this by first folding into halves, then into quarters and finally into eighths.

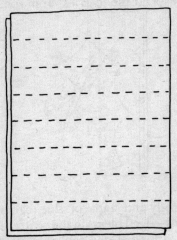

2 The result should look like this:

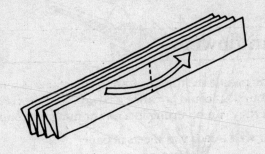

Fold in half.

3 With the folded edge at the bottom, cut through all layers at the top at an angle of at least 45° from the vertical.

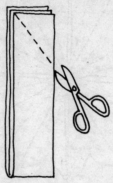

4 Open slightly and staple or glue together the tips of the two raw-edged pleats in the centre. This makes a fan — an attractive decoration in itself. Make a similar fan from a second sheet of paper and fasten their corners together.

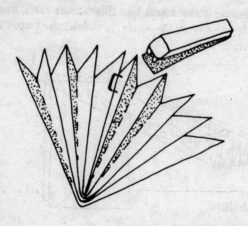

5 This is the result.

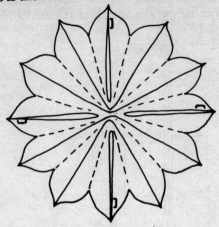

Christmas cards

Cut-out cards

1 The simplest way to make a Christmas card, from a small sheet of writing-paper, is to fold the paper in half like this:

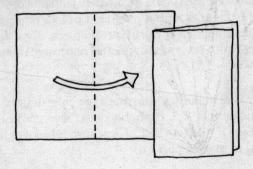

2 But it will feel more like a card, being firmer, if you use one of the larger sizes of writing-paper (A4 or foolscap) and fold it in half, first one way and then the other, like this:

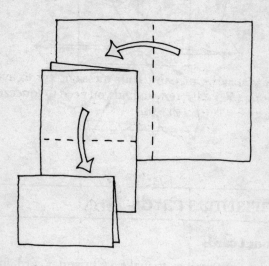

You can decorate such a card either with one of your own drawings, or with a photo cut from a magazine perhaps. One idea is to cut out pictures, or parts of pictures, from several sources and rearrange them in a new way.

3 You can make up your message from letters cut from magazines. It is probably better if you do not try to line up the letters neatly, but instead move them around to make a pattern.

4 If you write or paint your message, try to avoid starting off boldly, only to find you need to squeeze in the last few letters like this:

5 One way to avoid squashing the letters is to count the number of letters in each line (five in 'Merry' and nine in 'Christmas'); then find the middle letter or letters and write these first, in the middle.

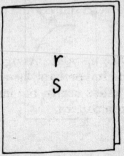

31

6 Then you can complete the words by adding letters from the middle outwards. If you still need to squeeze in letters, at least you will squeeze them in at both ends and so your lettering will look more balanced.

Cut-out cards

First fold the longer edges of a sheet of paper together. Make sure the folded edge is on the left.

1 Treat the folded edge as the centre and draw the right half of your design on the top layer.

2 Now cut around your design through both layers of paper.

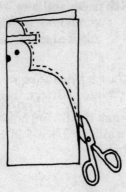

3 Open out the paper to see what the shape looks like. (You may need to refold the paper and trim off a bit more before you are really satisfied.) Complete the design with inks or paints. Write your message on the back of the card.

'Stained glass' card

You will need: paper and pencil
a craft knife or scissors
coloured tissue paper
glue

First fold all the edges of the paper together in turn to divide the sheet into quarters; then unfold.

1 Fill the bottom right-hand quarter with a drawing of a church window. Then fold the top half of the paper down behind.

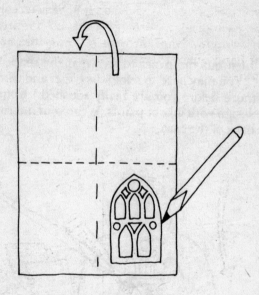

2 Cut out the shapes in the window, cutting through both layers. Now open up the paper.

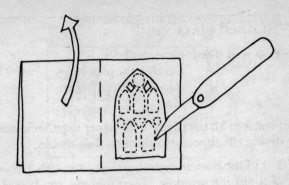

3 Prepare pieces of tissue paper of various colours, large enough to cover each of the cut-out areas in your window. Glue them in place on the bottom right-hand quarter; then close the card from top to bottom . . .

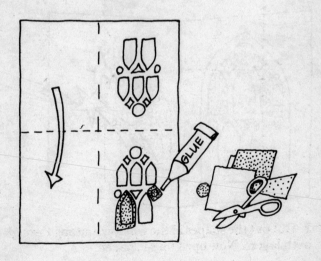

4 . . . and from left to right behind.

5 You have now finished the card, although you can make further decorations inside.

Simple crib

You will need: paper (A4 or foolscap)
scissors or a craft knife
sticky tape
a pencil
colouring materials

1 Fold the longer edges of the paper together to mark the centre line. Open up and cut along the crease to make two halves.

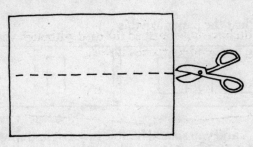

2 Fasten the two halves neatly together with sticky tape to make a long strip. Fold the ends of the strip to the centre join, crease and open up. Now the length is divided into four panels.

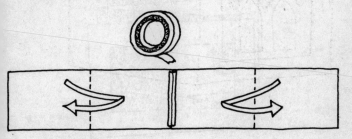

3 Starting from the left, cut a large window in the first panel; cut a window, about half as wide, to the left of the second panel; and cut a window, half as wide again, to the right of the third panel.

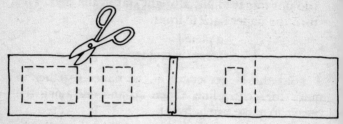

4 Pleat the paper like this . . .

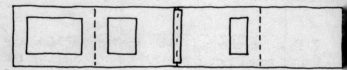

5 . . . and you should be able to see right through the big window and the smaller windows behind. This completes the basic structure of the simple crib. Now you can colour the various layers to make a three-dimensional picture.

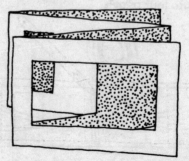

6 With the paper opened up, draw and colour Mary, Joseph and the baby Jesus in the second panel, close to the window. Make the fourth panel the background, with distant hills against a night sky (do not forget to put a bright star in the sky). Then turn the paper back to front.

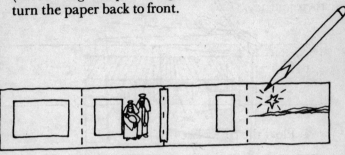

7 Draw shepherds in the second panel. Make the fourth panel (the frame) the surroundings of the stable, perhaps with a thatched roof and wooden walls.

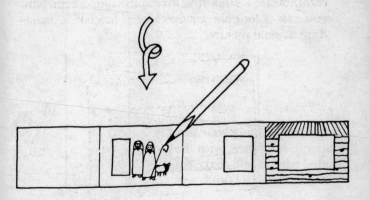

8 Pleat the paper again and consider the effect. You might want to make further cuts around the figures to open up the view. Think about putting in some animals, and what about drawing three little dots in the distant hills to represent the three wise men on their journey?

Angels

You will need: paper
scissors
colouring materials
glue or staples

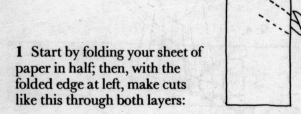

1 Start by folding your sheet of paper in half; then, with the folded edge at left, make cuts like this through both layers:

2 Open the paper and you will see the rough shape of an angel. Draw and colour the angel's head, wings and arms.

3 Now take the two side flaps behind and fasten them together to form the body.

GLUE

4 Bring the arms forward and put crimps in the wings to make them stand out more . . .

5 . . . like this:

6 You can make a carol sheet for the angel by folding a scrap of paper in half. Fix it to his hands with two spots of glue.

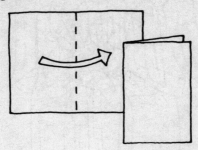

7 Or you can make a trumpet by rolling up a scrap of paper, keeping it pointed at one end.

8 Glue the loose corner to fix the shape and cut off the end.

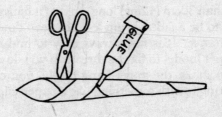

9 Try making a group of angels to represent a heavenly choir, singing and playing trumpets.

Angel mobile

Angels are particularly suitable subjects if you want to make a mobile – one of those hanging decorations which gently turn in the breeze.

You will need: angels
a needle and thread
lightweight rods (cane or wire)
scissors

Start by suspending an angel from a thread (not more than 30cm (12ins) long) so that it hangs at what seems to be a suitable angle – not head downwards, for instance. It is not always easy to find the right spot on a model to fix the thread. If you do not seem able to make the angel hang nicely, you could try weighting it with something like a paper-clip.

1 Thread up a second angel and suspend them both by looping their threads over either end of a rod about 30—40cm (12—16ins) long. Tie a thread to the centre of the rod and adjust its position so that the rod remains level when you hold the thread. Fix it to the ceiling and you have a simple mobile.

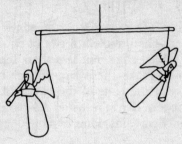

2 Make a second mobile as above, using a longer rod. Hang the first mobile from it. You can add to your mobile, one unit at a time, working from the bottom upwards. Remember to check the balance of each unit as you progress – and make sure you give the angels enough space so that they will not bump into each other when the rods turn.

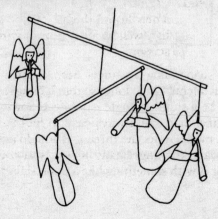

Japanese lantern

You will need: paper (A4 or foolscap)
a pencil and ruler
scissors
sticky tape

1 Start by folding the two shorter edges of your paper together. Then make a series of equi-distant cuts into the folded edge, not less than 1cm (½in) apart. You *must* make these cuts longer than the distance between the ends of the cuts and the top edge of the paper. If you're using A4 paper, make your cuts about 8cm (3ins) long, or a bit longer. Then unfold.

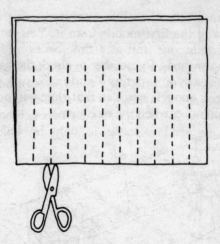

2 Fold the paper forward at the top and bottom of the cuts.

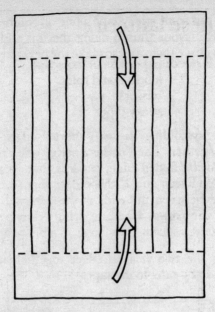

3 Put some sticky tape along the bottom raw edge of the paper; then bring the two edges together so that they stick to the tape side by side. (The strips behind will bend as you do this so the paper will not lie flat; you may need someone to help by holding the paper.)

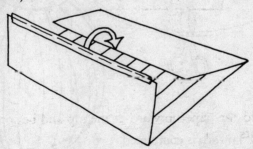

4 Now put some sticky tape along one of the vertical edges. Run your thumb along the top and bottom edges to curve them and so make the next part easier.

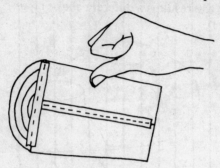

5 Bring the two vertical edges together and stick them, side by side, to the tape.

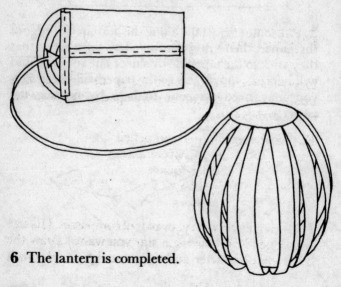

6 The lantern is completed.

7 If you make longer cuts at the outset, the lantern will be shorter and squatter. If, in step **2,** you place the horizontal folds 1–2cm (½in) above and below the cuts, the result is a different shape again.

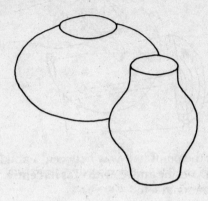

Christmas stars

Here is a method of constructing an accurate five-pointed star which can be developed in various ways to make decorations.

You will need: paper and pencil
a pair of compasses
a set-square
a ruler
scissors

1 Draw a circle with your pair of compasses. (Its size will depend on how big a star you want.) Draw the horizontal diameter and a line at right angles to it from the centre. Let us call the centre point A and the point at right, where the diameter meets the circumference, B.

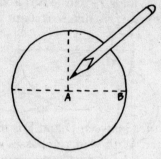

2 Find the point half-way between A and B and call this C. Describe an arc, with C as its centre, from D to the diameter at left.

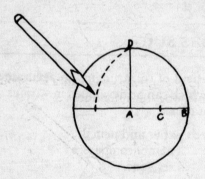

3 Call this point E. Describe an arc, with D as centre, to a point on the circumference. Call this point F.

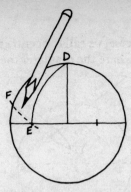

4 The distance between D and F is one-fifth of the circumference. With your compasses still set at this distance, divide the circumference into fifths.

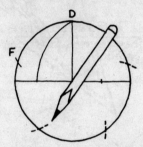

5 Then join up these points to form a five-pointed star shape. Cut along the outer lines . . .

6 . . . to complete.

7 If you cut holes in your star like this . . .

8 . . . you can then cover them with pieces of coloured tissue-paper or acetate.

9 Turn the star over and hang in the window (or somewhere else where light will shine through from behind) for an attractive stained-glass effect.

10 Instead of cutting out the star itself, try cutting out the circle which contains the star. Then make a cut from the circumference to each angle between the points.

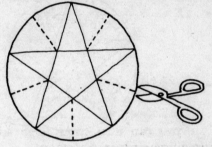

11 Curl the corners in front and behind each point . . .

12 . . . to make this crossed horns decoration.

13 Another idea is to cut lines between the points of the star.

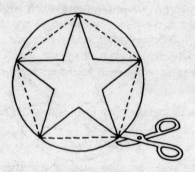

14 Then cut lines to the edges of the star . . .

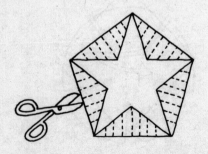

15 . . . and curl the little flaps forward for this decorative effect.

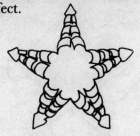

Cut-out Christmas trees

These trees, made from coloured squares of paper, become attractive ornaments when arranged on a mantelpiece or sideboard. After making the basic tree, the two variations and the frilly tree, try developing your own ideas with papers of various colours.

You will need: squares of coloured paper
scissors
sticky tape

1 Fold two opposite corners together; make a firm crease and unfold.

2 Fold the top edges in turn to the centre crease.

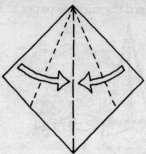

3 Fold the raw edges outwards to meet the folded edges. Then turn the paper over.

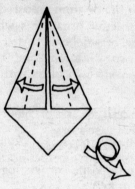

4 Fold the left and right folded edges to the centre crease.

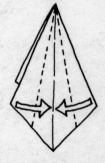

5 Cut through all layers just below the horizontal edge and discard the surplus paper at bottom.

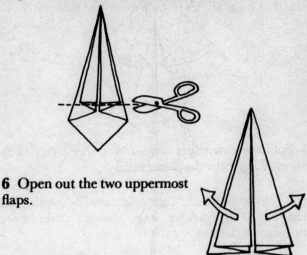

6 Open out the two uppermost flaps.

7 Fasten a strip of sticky tape along the left edge, overlapping it. Close the left flap; then close the right flap on to the overlapping sticky paper. This should fasten the two edges together neatly.

8 You now have a tall, narrow, triangular structure with a pair of flaps at left and right. Make the flaps stand at right angles to each other like this . . .

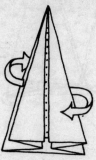

9 . . . to make a basic Christmas tree. By cutting into the paper in various ways we can make more decorative designs.

Variation 1

1 Complete the basic Christmas tree. Make a series of horizontal cuts in the right-hand flap, from the outer edge to the vertical centre line, to create branches.

2 Fold every second branch
across to the left.

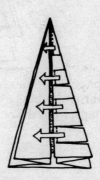

3 Let one of the triangular flaps project behind to
support the completed tree.

Variation 2

1 Complete the basic Christmas tree. Fold the edges of the uppermost left and right flaps in turn to the centre. Crease lightly and return.

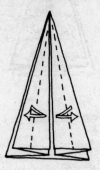

2 Make two or more cuts, at left and right, through both flaps, from the outer edges to the crease lines.

3 Fold the paper below each cut at an angle as shown. Turn the paper over and fold on the other side too. Then let the flaps stand at right angles to each other . . .

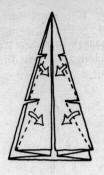

4 . . . like this.

Frilly Christmas tree

You will need: three large sheets of writing-paper
(A4 or foolscap)
a pencil and ruler
a pair of compasses
scissors
glue

1 With your pair of compasses, draw five circles with radii of 8, 7, 6, 5 and 4cm (3.1, 2.7, 2.3, 1.9, 1.5ins) respectively. Cut neatly around these circles to make five paper discs.

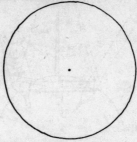

2 On each disc, draw two radii at right angles to each other.

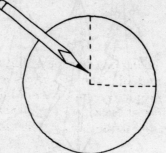

3 Cut along one of these lines on each disc.

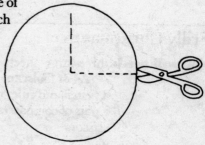

4 Draw a concentric circle (i.e. a circle with the same centre as the disc) within each disc with a radius half as long as the radius of the disc. Glue the area between the slit and the drawn radial line.

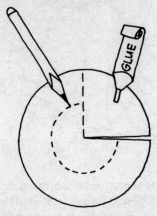

5 Overlap, taking one edge of the slit to the drawn radial line, and stick the two layers together. This raises each disc into a cup shape. Make a series of radiating cuts, at least 1cm (½in) apart, from the edge of each disc to the drawn circle inside the cup.

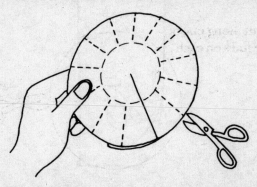

6 Run the end of each little flap in turn carefully between your thumb and the scissor-blade to make it curl. This completes a set of five tiers of leaves.

7 To make the trunk, take a large sheet of writing-paper cut in half lengthways (about 10 × 30cm (4 × 12ins)) and roll it up. Start by curling one corner and roll the paper so that one end is narrower than the other. Make the narrow end as pointed as you can.

8 Open the narrow end a little, apply glue and close it again to fasten.

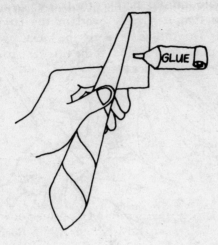

9 Now take the largest tier of leaves and cut a little hole at the top. You may need to squeeze and flatten the paper to do this.

10 Slip this tier of leaves over the trunk and slide it down about half-way. Take the next largest tier, cut a little hole and slip this over the trunk too, pulling it down so that it slightly overlaps the largest tier beneath. Do the same with the next two tiers. Finally, put a spot of glue on the tip of the trunk and fasten the smallest tier to it.

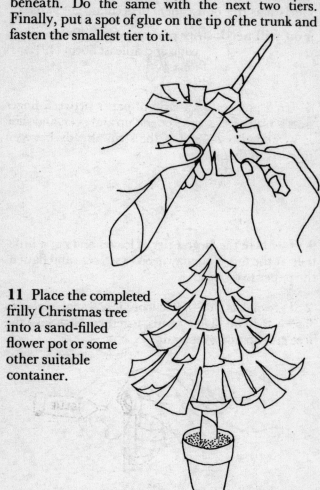

11 Place the completed frilly Christmas tree into a sand-filled flower pot or some other suitable container.

Coil decorations

You can either hang these on the branches of a Christmas tree or use them to decorate gift parcels.

You will need: strips of strong paper, 1–2cm (½in) wide and at least 50cm (19½ins) long
glue

1 Hold one end of a strip of paper between finger and thumb. Bring the free end up and over, and slide it behind the top end of the strip already between finger and thumb.

2 This makes a complete loop. Use a spot of glue to fasten the two layers neatly together. Now take the free end up and over again . . .

3 . . . and slide it behind the first loop, again using a spot of glue to fasten the two layers together. Let this loop stand out from the first loop in front. Make more loops in the same way, each standing out about the same distance from the previous one . . .

4 . . . like this. (You should be able to make at least five loops with a 50cm (19½ins) strip. If you find you have *less* than five, try again, making your loops a little tighter this time. It is all right to have *more* than five loops.) Use a spot of glue on the end of the strip to fasten it and fix the shape of the coil.

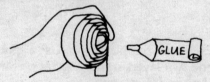

5 The coil is now complete. You can use it in this form as a simple decoration, or pinch and squeeze it in various ways to make other decorative shapes.

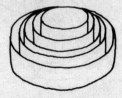

6 For example, if you pinch the coil on the side of the smallest loop, then push the opposite side with finger and thumb . . .

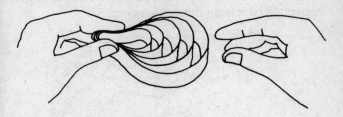

7 . . . spreading the loops and pressing them against the finger and thumb of your other hand . . . .

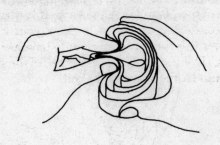

8 . . . when released, the coil should take the form of a bell.

9 But if you pinch the opposite side of the coil, and press against the smallest loop, pushing it right down . . .

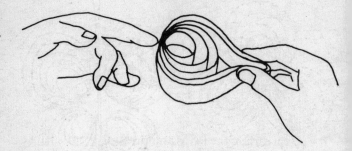

10 . . . you should get a form resembling a heart. See what other forms you can discover by pinching and squeezing.

11 Try making several coils and fixing them together with a little glue to create new shapes. Add shorter strips of paper if this helps the design. Three coils joined together will form a shamrock design if a strip, folded in half, is added to represent the stem. Two pairs of coils, one a little larger than the other, can be used to make an attractive butterfly design. A doubled strip of paper, with ends curled, forms the body and antennae.

Two party hats

You can make these hats from ordinary newspaper or, perhaps, newspaper painted with stripes as described on page 9. In either case you will need to start by cutting the newspaper into a square. This is how to do it:

1 Take a sheet of paper and fold a short edge to a longer edge. Make a sharp crease.

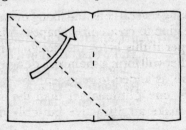

2 Cut along the vertical edge of the triangle. Then unfold . . .

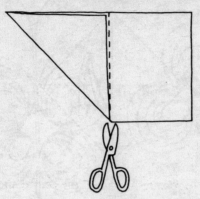

3 . . . and you have a square.

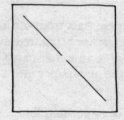

Crown

You will need: paper about 40cm (16ins) square. Make this, as shown on page 71, using a double page from a small (tabloid) newspaper or a single page from a large (broadsheet) newspaper.

1 Start by folding opposite corners together in turn, creasing firmly and unfolding. This will mark the centre of the square.

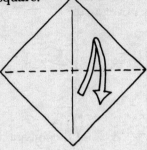

2 Fold two opposite corners to the centre and crease firmly. Turn the paper over.

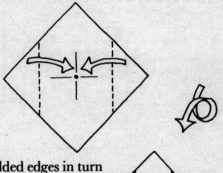

3 Lift the folded edges in turn and fold them to the centre; at the same time...

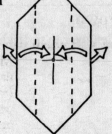

4 . . . letting the points stick out like this:

Turn the paper over again.

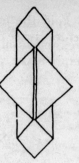

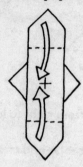

5 Fold the top and bottom points to the centre . . .

6 . . . like this. Turn the paper over.

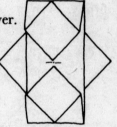

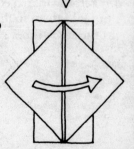

7 Turn the large triangular flap at left over to the right.

8 Fold the top and bottom corners at left to the centre crease line.

9 Take both large triangular flaps from right to left.

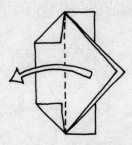

10 Fold the top and bottom corners at right to the centre crease line; then return the uppermost large flap to the right.

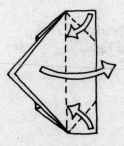

11 Put your thumbs into the centre pocket and pull the sides apart.

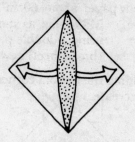

12 The four points will rise to form a crown.

Mitre

You will need: paper about 60cm (24ins) square. Make this, as shown on page 71, using a double page from a large (broadsheet) newspaper.

1 Start by folding the bottom corner to the top and making a firm crease.

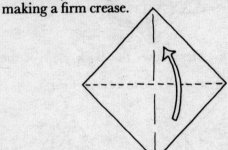

2 Fold up the paper 2–3cm (1in) from the bottom edge on a line parallel to it.

3 Fold the left corner across to the right . . .

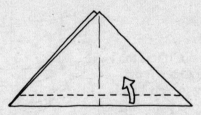

4 . . . and the right corner across to the left, tucking the point of one into the pocket of the other . . .

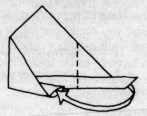

5 . . . like this. This shows the back view of the completed mitre.

6 Try it on. If it is too loose, you can tighten it by returning to step 4 and pushing one point further into its opposite pocket.

78

Making fancy papers

Perhaps you would like to make your own patterned paper – something you could use for wrapping your gifts. Although making detailed repeat patterns can be boring if you have to paint them, it can be fun if you employ one of the easier and quicker methods of decoration described below.

Why not try each of the methods on a small sheet of paper first? You can use these smaller patterned papers as greeting cards, folding them in half and pasting cut-out pictures on the covers. Doing this may also help you decide which method you would most like to try again – next time on a larger scale.

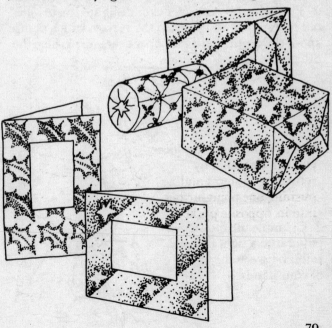

'Leatherette' paper

You will need: paper

water-colour paint (powder or tube)

a brush (about 2–3cm (1in) wide is best)

a sponge or cloth

an old newspaper

a saucer

a sink or wash-basin with tap

First prepare the paint by mixing it with water in the saucer to make a coloured 'wash'; that is to say, the mixture should be watery rather than creamy.

1 Place the sheet of paper to be decorated on to some old newspaper and moisten the surface with a damp sponge or cloth. Turn the paper over and moisten the other side too.

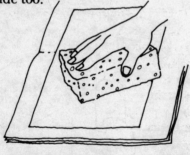

2 Crumple the moistened paper into a tight ball and roll it between the palms of your hands.

3 Now carefully unfold the ball of paper and lay it on the old newspaper again. Lightly brush the colour wash on to the paper, covering the surface.

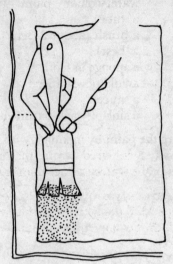

4 Then hold the paper under a tap to wash off some of the colour – allow the colour to remain mostly in the cracks. Lay on old newspaper to dry.

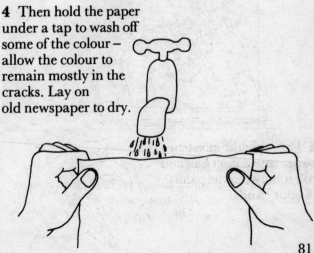

5 The completed paper should be covered with a web of fine coloured lines and look a bit like leather. You might try applying two colours to your paper, one colour blending into the other, to get a more interesting effect.

Speckled paper

You will need: paper
water-colour paint (or food colours)
an old toothbrush
an old newspaper

1 Dip the old toothbrush in water-colour paint or food colour . . .

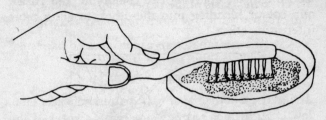

2 . . . and rub your thumb along it so that paint spatters over the paper. (Make sure you have put plenty of old newspaper underneath it to protect the furniture.)

That is all there is to it. Speckling paper is easy to do, but perhaps not so easy to do really well. Try making clusters of speckles in one part of the paper and be more sparing in others.

It is best to limit yourself to just one or two colours. Too many differently coloured speckles on the paper may turn into a nasty, muddy colour. Experiment with metallic colours if you can; silver or gold speckles on blue paper can look like a starry sky.

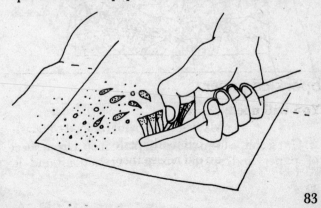

Patterns in speckled paper

By covering parts of the paper before speckling, you can create a variety of more controlled patterns.

You will need: materials as for speckled paper
thin card
scissors

1 Cover all of the paper to be patterned, except for a few cm (an inch) at one side, with a sheet of thin card. Spatter paint along the edge of the card. Remove it and you should find a sort of stripe on the paper – hard-edged on one side and misty on the other. Uncover more of the paper and make a second stripe in the same way. Continue until your paper is covered with such stripes.

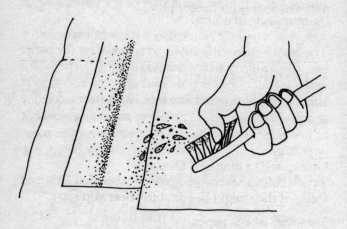

2 Cut a shape from the card, place it on a fresh sheet of paper and spatter paint over and around it.

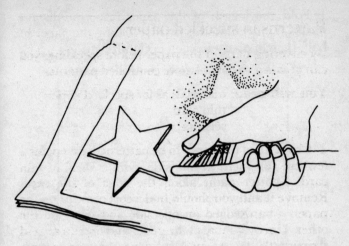

Remove the cut-out shape carefully to reveal an image of it on the paper. Repeat until your paper is patterned with similar shapes.

Dip-and-dye paper

It is important to use fairly thin, absorbent paper for this project to be successful – not paper as absorbent as ordinary tissues, but more absorbent than some papers generally used for writing and drawing, e.g. kitchen roll or man-size tissues.

Try to collect several samples of paper that look and feel as if they might be suitable before you start.

You will need: paper
food colours
a small container for the colour
an old newspaper

1 Fold the length of the paper into equi-distant pleats. You can do this by first folding the paper in half, then in quarters, then in eighths, etc. . . .

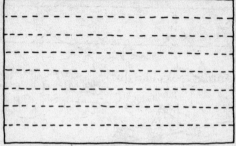

2 . . . like this:

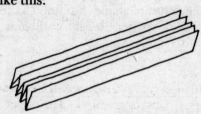

3 Fold the end of the pleated strip to the top edge.

4 Then fold the triangular area behind.

5 Fold the new end down to the bottom edge; then fold the triangular area back. Repeat these steps along the pleated strip . . .

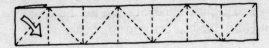

6 . . . until it looks like this.

7 Put some food colour into a small container, such as an egg cup. Compress the folded paper in your hand and dip one corner of it into the colour. Remove almost immediately.

8 Press the coloured corner between two sheets of newspaper to spread the dye more evenly. Dip the other two corners to colour them too. You could try dipping one of them into the same dye, holding the paper at a slightly different angle this time, or dip the second and third corner into other colours.

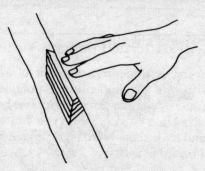

9 Unfold the paper carefully, to find what sort of pattern you have made, and lay it on a newspaper to

dry. If the result is not good – if the paper has not absorbed the colour properly – try again with different paper. On the other hand, if the paper is almost covered with dye so that there is not enough definition between the different shapes, that means you probably held the paper in the dye too long.   .

Potato-cut patterned paper

Potato-cutting is sometimes thought of as a poor man's substitute for lino-cutting, potatoes being easier to come by than squares of lino. It is best to cut potatoes with lino-cutting tools (you can get these from art and craft shops) but, if you do not have any of these, a penknife will do.

You will need: paper
a medium-sized potato
a small knife
lino-cutting tools (optional)
water-colour paints
a saucer

1 Cut the potato neatly in half. Do not hack at it – you will need a smooth surface where it has been cut.

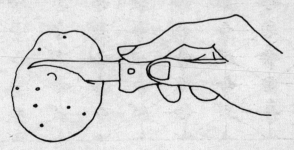

2 Take one half of the potato and prick out a design on the smooth surface with your knife.

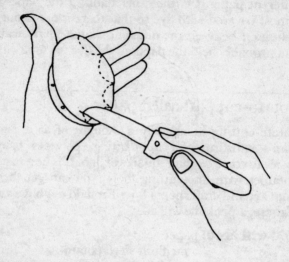

3 Now make further cuts until your design stands out from the background – you have cut away the parts you do not want to print.

4 Mix up plenty of paint in a saucer and press your potato half into it.

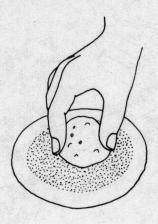

5 Then transfer the potato to your paper and press it down firmly. Lift it, and an impression of your design should appear on the paper.

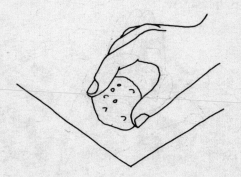

6 Make more prints with your potato, working to some sort of plan. Try making a row of prints in one colour followed by a row of prints in another colour, and so on . . .

7 . . . or make your second row of prints stand at a different angle to the first. Whatever you do, try to place the prints close together; do not just spot them about on the paper.

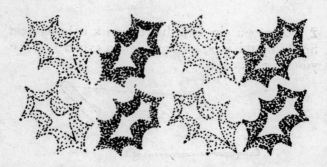

Festive candles

A few craft shops specialize in candle-making equipment. You can find wax in many different colours there.

You will need: a sheet of beeswax (from a craft shop)

wicking (from a craft shop)

a knife or scissors

gold or silver glitter (optional)

1 Place the sheet of beeswax on a smooth surface. Lay the wicking across it, about 1cm (½in) from the near edge. Cut the wicking to leave 4–5 cm (1½–2in) of wick projecting over the side. Turn the near edge of the wax over the wick and press it down.

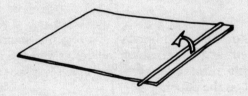

2 When you are sure that the wick is being held firmly by the wax, roll it up into a cylinder. When you have done this . . .

3 . . . you will have a candle. If you have some glitter, scatter a little on a sheet of paper and roll the candle in it. The wax will pick it up.

4 This gives the candle a truly festive appearance.

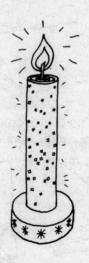

Helter-skelter candles

You will need: materials as for the festive candle (i.e. a sheet of beeswax, wicking, a knife or scissors, optional gold or silver glitter)
a ruler or straight-edge

1 Place the sheet of beeswax on a smooth surface. Measure 2–3cm (1in) along the shorter edges from opposite corners. Draw a line between the two points with your knife or scissors. Cut along this line to separate the wax into two halves.

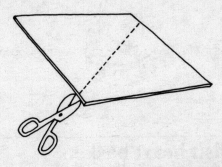

2 Lay the wicking 1cm (½in) from the near edge and proceed as for the festive candle (page 93). Make a second, matching candle from the other half of the beeswax.

3 The completed candle tapers towards the top. The line of the edge running around it makes it look like a helter-skelter.

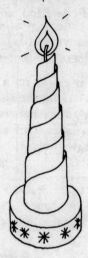

Danish heart baskets

Heart-shaped baskets, such as the one shown below, are traditionally made in Denmark at Christmas time.

You will need: two sheets of paper, preferably of different colours (e.g. white and red)

scissors

a pencil and ruler

glue

1 Prepare two rectangles of paper, 6 × 18cm (2½ × 7ins), and a strip, 1.5 × 18cm (½ × 7ins). Place the two 6 × 18cm rectangles together and fold them in half. Fold the strip in half, too, and put this aside for the moment.

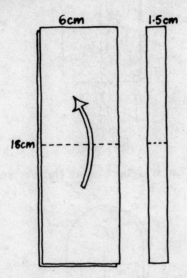

2 Draw a full, rounded curve at the top. Raise a vertical line, 6cm (2½ins) long, from the centre of the bottom edge.

3 Now cut along the pencilled lines and separate the two pieces.

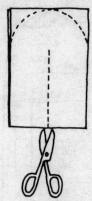

4 Arrange the two pieces (call them A and B) like this:

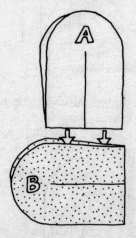

Tuck one of the flaps of piece A between the two layers of piece B.

5 Bring piece A down further, pulling the inside flap out through the slit in piece B.

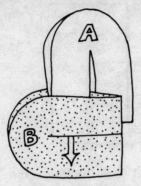

6 Pull the top flap of piece B to the left . . .

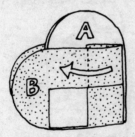

7 . . . and bring the long flap of piece A to the front.

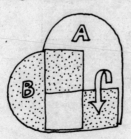

8 Tuck the top flap of piece B between the layers of the long flap of piece A. Then take the bottom flap of piece B from behind to the left . . .

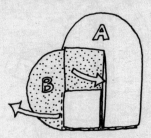

9 . . . and bring it back, tucking it into the pocket made by the left flap of piece A. Raise the right flap of piece A . . .

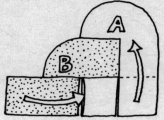

10 . . . and tuck it into the bottom flap of piece B.

11 You now have a heart-shaped basket. Press the edges to open it. Glue each end of the paper strip to the insides to make a handle.

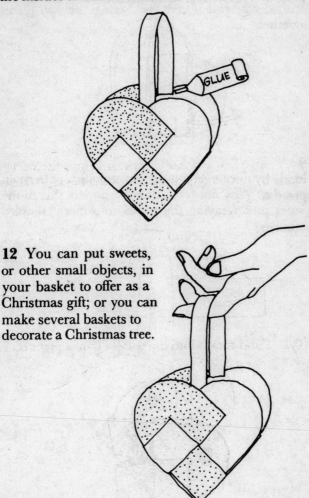

12 You can put sweets, or other small objects, in your basket to offer as a Christmas gift; or you can make several baskets to decorate a Christmas tree.

13 If, having prepared your two rectangles of paper and folded them in half, you cut three 6cm (2½ins) slits, 1.5cm (½in) apart, instead of cutting one central slit; and if you then weave the two pieces together . . .

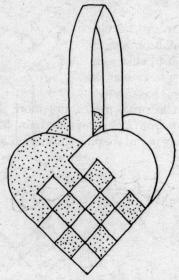

14 . . . you can get a heart basket with a pattern on its sides. Why not try cutting even more slits in the paper and weaving the pieces into more complex patterns?

Things to eat

Marzipan fruits

You will need: marzipan
food colours
a dish of water
a small water-colour brush
clove stems
a grater
a knife

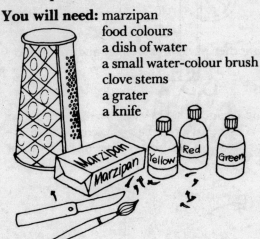

1 Cut several small pieces, not more than 2–3cm (1in) square, from a block of marzipan. Model one of these, pulling it and shaping the ends . . .

2 . . . to make a banana. Paint it yellow. Mix a little red and green colour with water and paint lines on it with this.

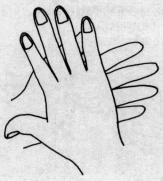

3 Take another piece of marzipan and roll it into a ball.

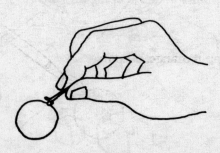

4 Push a clove stem into the top . . .

5 . . . and paint it green and red to look like an apple.

6 Make another marzipan ball and roll it on the finest part of the grater. This roughens the surface and gives it the texture of an orange.

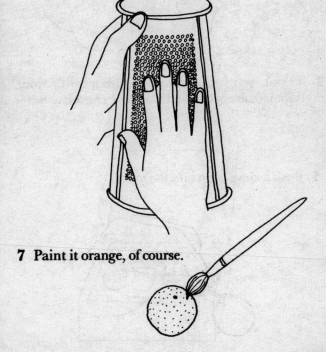

7 Paint it orange, of course.

8 You can make a pear by first rolling a ball of marzipan and then stretching one end. Paint it yellow and green.

To represent a strawberry, make a marzipan ball and roll it on the medium part of the grater. This gives it the indented surface of a strawberry. Paint it red. Shape leaves from flakes of marzipan and paint them green before pressing them on one end.

9 If you want to present someone with your marzipan fruits, try to find an empty chocolate box –

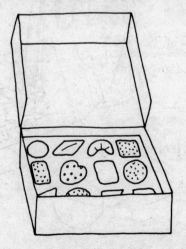

particularly one with a lining inside with impressed shapes which once held the chocolates. Your fruits will look very special if you lay them out in a box like this. You can cover any inappropriate lettering on the outside of the box with one of your fancy papers (pages 79–92).

Fondant creams

'Fondant' comes from the French word for 'melt'. It is a word sometimes used to describe sweets which start to melt as soon as you put them on your tongue. Try these and see.

You will need: 225g (8oz) of icing sugar
          a sieve
          1 egg
          food colours and flavouring
          a bowl
          1 or more cups
          greaseproof paper
          a knife and fork

1 Tip the icing sugar into a bowl. Sieve first to remove any lumps.

2 Take an egg and separate the white from the yolk. Do this by breaking the egg neatly in two (without breaking the yolk), holding the two halves together over a cup and allowing only the white of the egg to drop into the cup. Pass the yolk from one half of the eggshell to the other so that you can get out a bit more of the white. Put the yolk aside as it is not needed for this project. (Perhaps you can have it poached or fried later.)

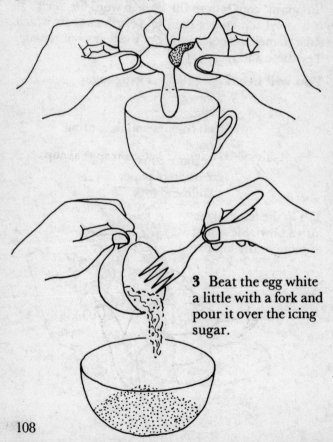

3 Beat the egg white a little with a fork and pour it over the icing sugar.

4 Mix the two together to make a thick, sticky cream. When well mixed, you can add one or two drops of food colour and flavouring (such as vanilla, cherry, peppermint, etc.) to the mixture in the bowl – or, if you have several colours and flavours available . . .

5 . . . divide the mixture between several cups . . .

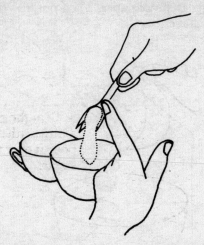

6 . . . and add a drop of different colour and different flavour to each. Mix the contents of each cup thoroughly.

7 Drop the creamy mixture in soft lumps on to a sheet of greaseproof paper. Then put into the fridge until they have set.

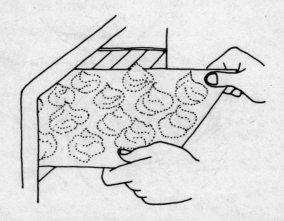

8 After two hours, check whether the creams are still sticky. If you can cut cleanly through one of the lumps with a knife, without the cream sticking to the blade, it is time to remove them from the fridge. Flatten each one by pressing the top with the side of your knife so that none is more than 1cm (½in) thick.

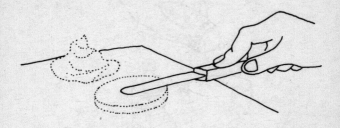

9 Then cut and mould them into shapes.

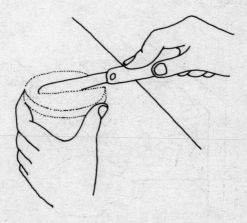

10 As well as simple shapes, such as squares and diamonds, try more seasonal designs such as Christmas trees and Father Christmas' boots.

Coconut snowballs and snowman

You will need: 55g (2oz) desiccated coconut
55g (2oz) sultanas (or other dried fruit)
55g (2oz) almonds (or other nuts)
55g (2oz) biscuits (plain, such as digestive)
75cc (2.5fl.oz) fresh cream
a bowl
a board
a rolling-pin
a knife, fork and spoon
paper or plastic bag
a measuring-jug

1 Crumble the biscuits by rolling them with a rolling-pin.

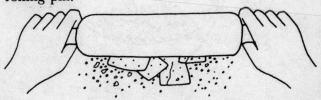

2 Chop the nuts and fruit into small pieces.

3 Put the crumbled biscuits, chopped nuts and fruit into a bowl; then add the cream.

4 Mix well.

5 Mould the mixture
into small balls . . .

6 . . . and drop them, a few at a time, into a bag
containing the desiccated coconut.

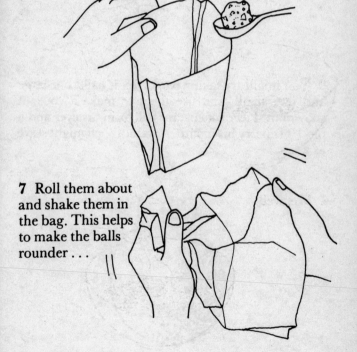

7 Roll them about
and shake them in
the bag. This helps
to make the balls
rounder . . .

8 . . . and when you take them out they should be covered in coconut. They are ready to eat straight away.

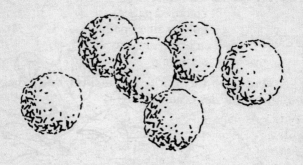

9 You might try taking two coconut balls, one large and one small, and use them to make a coconut snowman. Pieces of currant will form his eyes and a piece of cherry his mouth. A walnut shell might serve as a hat.

Fir-cone flowers

You will need: a fir-cone
coloured paper
gold or silver paint
a brush or spray
scissors
glue

1 First brush or
spray a fir-cone
with gold or silver
paint.

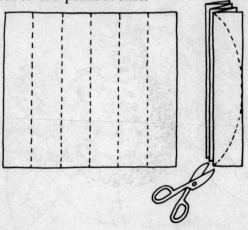

2 Cut petal shapes (a bit longer than the cone) from
scraps of coloured paper. If you pleat the paper, you
can cut several petals at once.

3 Open and curl the ends of the petals.

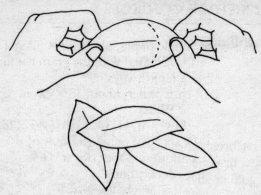

4 Put a spot of glue on the end of each petal and arrange them around the cone, tucking the glued ends in between the scales. The petals should overlap each other slightly and form at least one circle. If you like, you can make a second circle of petals above the first, using a different shade of coloured paper. Try arranging your fir-cone flowers with bunches of real holly to make a decoration for the dinner-table.

Christmas crackers

You will need: crêpe paper, about 18 × 32cm (7 × 12½ins) with the grain running lengthways

thin paper, about 16 × 30cm (6 × 12ins)

thin card, 11.5 × 15cm (4½ × 6ins)

a scrap of paper (for motto)

coloured paper (for surface decoration)

three empty toilet-rolls

sticky tape

string

glue

a ruler

a small gift

a 'snap' (to make the bang)

If you want your cracker to bang you will have to put in a 'snap' which you can buy from specialist suppliers of novelties. However, if you just want a rather special wrapping for a small gift, why not use a cracker without the snap.

1 Fasten two empty toilet-rolls together, end to end, with sticky tape. You will need these along with a third roll, to help form the container later.

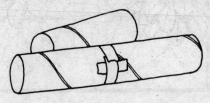

2 Take the 18 × 32cm crêpe paper and run the shorter edges between thumb and finger in a series of outward pulling movements. Do not grasp the paper or it will tear; just let the paper slide between your thumb and finger as you work your way down each edge. This will make the edges frilly.

3 Lay the crêpe paper on a flat surface. Place the 16 × 30cm thin paper on it in the centre, but with the bottom edges meeting. Place your motto (it does not have to be a motto; it may be a joke, riddle or poem) in the centre and lay the snap, if you have one, across it.

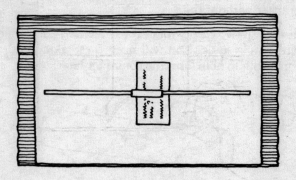

4 Place the 11.5 × 15cm thin card in the centre, but with a shorter edge meeting the bottom edges of the other papers. Glue along the top edge of the crêpe paper.

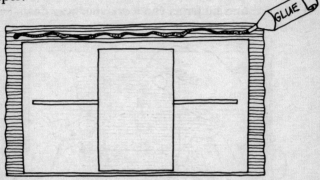

5 Place the double toilet-roll on the paper, so that one end of the roll meets the right edge of the thin card.

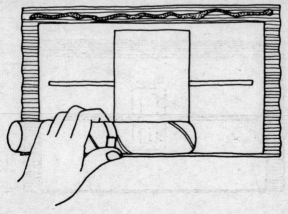

6 Bring the third toilet-roll to meet it. Now treat them as óne continuous tube; roll up the tube, taking the paper with it so that the paper becomes tightly wrapped around it. When you get to the top, firmly stick the rolled paper to the glued edge.

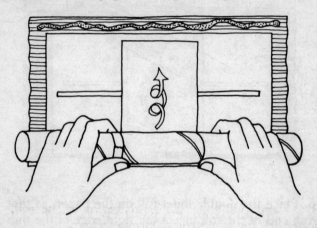

7 Pull out the right-hand toilet-roll about 4cm (1½ins).

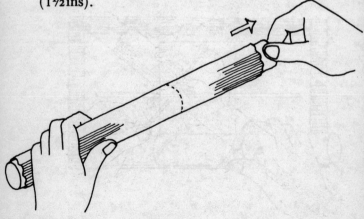

8 Lay a piece of string underneath the rolled paper midway between the two toilet-rolls. Bring the ends up and across . . .

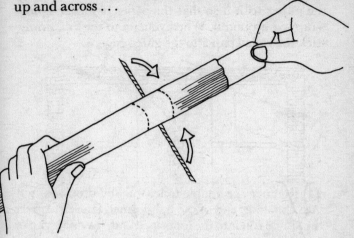

9 . . . and pull them, at right angles to the roll, squeezing the paper and so forming a neck.

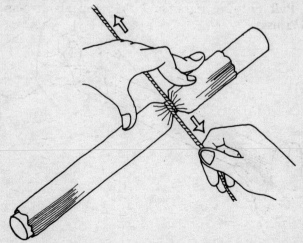

10 Remove the string and give the neck a twist to complete one end.

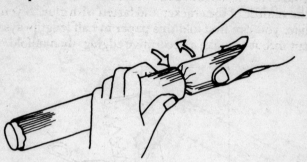

11 Remove the double toilet-roll and drop your gift into this long end of the half-formed cracker. Insert the single roll into the unformed end, leaving a gap of 4cm (1½ins) between the end of the roll and the edge of the thin card inside. Then repeat steps **8, 9** and **10** to complete the basic construction of the cracker.

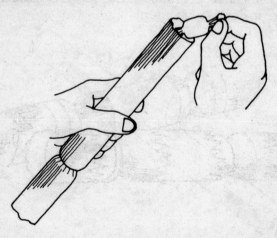

12 Wrap coloured or fancy paper, or paper-backed gold or silver foil, about 8 × 15cm (3 × 6ins), around the middle of the cracker and fasten with glue. If you like, you can first fold this paper in half lengthways, cut into it to make a decorative edging, then unfold.

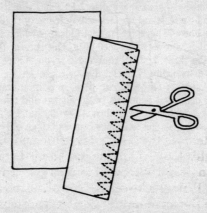

13 The cracker is complete. Use scraps of coloured paper to decorate the ends.

BODY MAGIC

Peter Eldin

A collection of amazing stunts, tricks and activities designed to help you understand the delicate machinery that makes up the human body. There are optical illusions which the reader can try which show how the eyes and brain function; also balancing skills, tests of touch and so on. There are also some pretty extraordinary facts. Few people know, for instance, that a piece of skin the size of a 5p coin contains over three million cells, one hundred sweat glands and twenty-five nerve endings or that we have about 100,000 hairs on our heads or that a young person has more bones than an old.

ERIC KENNEWAY

If you're an eager Beaver reader, perhaps you ought to try some more of our exciting Eric Kenneway titles. They are available in bookshops or they can be ordered directly from us. Just complete the form below and enclose the right amount of money and the books will be sent to you.

☐	PAPER FUN	£1.00
☐	PAPER SHAPES	95p
☐	FINGERS, KNUCKLES AND THUMBS	90p
☐	MAGIC TOYS, TRICKS AND ILLUSIONS	95p
☐	MORE MAGIC TOYS, TRICKS AND ILLUSIONS	£1.25
☐	THE HORROR'S HANDBOOK	95p
☐	THE RUBBER BAND BOOK	£1.00

And if you would like to hear more about Beaver Books, and find out all the latest news, don't forget the Beaver Bulletin. Just send a stamped, self-addressed envelope to Beaver Books, 62 – 65 Chandos Place, Covent Garden, London WC2N 4NW and we will send you one.

If you would like to order books, please send this form with the money due to:

HAMLYN PAPERBACK CASH SALES, PO BOX 11, FALMOUTH, CORNWALL TR10 9EN

Send a cheque or postal order, and don't forget to include postage at the following rates: UK: 55p for the first book, 22p for the second, 14p for each additional book; BFPO and Eire: 55p for the first book, 22p for the second, 14p for the next seven books and 8p per book thereafter. Overseas: £1.00 for first book and 25p for each additional book.

NAME..

ADDRESS..

....

Please print clearly